Clifford Lake Inn

✠✠

Compiled and Edited
by
Gary L. Hauck

iUniverse, Inc.
Bloomington

Clifford Lake Inn

iUniverse books may be ordered through booksellers or by contacting:

iUniverse
1663 Liberty Drive
Bloomington, IN 47403
www.iuniverse.com
1-800-Authors (1-800-288-4677)

Because of the dynamic nature of the Internet, any web addresses or links contained in this book may have changed since publication and may no longer be valid. The views expressed in this work are solely those of the author and do not necessarily reflect the views of the publisher, and the publisher hereby disclaims any responsibility for them.

Any people depicted in stock imagery provided by Thinkstock are models, and such images are being used for illustrative purposes only.

Certain stock imagery © Thinkstock.

ISBN: 978-1-4759-3056-6 (sc)
ISBN: 978-1-4759-3057-3 (e)

Printed in the United States of America

iUniverse rev. date: 6/04/2012

Contents

Preface

It was in the summer of 2008 when I enjoyed my first dining experience at Clifford Lake Inn. Because I was the "new kid on the block" in the administration of Montcalm Community College, the school's vice president treated me and other members of the staff at the quaint, waterside establishment. Later that fall, I attended the Leadership Montcalm banquet at the Inn along with other leaders from the greater Montcalm Area. And in the spring, I was invited to speak at the annual awards banquet of Central Montcalm High School, sponsored by the Stanton Rotary Club.

Obviously, this soon came to be one of my favorite eateries of choice in Montcalm County. So, it came as no surprise when concert pianist and recording artist, Bob Milne, requested on show night at Montcalm Heritage Village, "Please take me to Clifford Lake Inn!"

Bob Milne at Clifford Lake Inn, with his wife, Linda, mother-in-law Carolyn Leithauser, Marilyn and Jesse Fox, and Lois Hauck.

This has turned into another annual tradition. During our 2011 dinner together, Milne explained his most recent composition – a full opera titled, *The Legend of Sleepy Hollow.* Through these many experiences, I've come to love this historic landmark during all seasons of the year – surrounded by spring flowers, witnessing the summer lake activities, set against the backdrop of autumn's blazing colors, or glittering with holiday decorations in the winter snow.

During the early fall of 2011, I learned that the Inn's new owner, Connie McKeown, envisioned a memoir of the Inn's history to celebrate its 130th anniversary. I had just written a brief history of the Montcalm Heritage Village in Sidney, Michigan (*The Story of Heritage Village*), and several suggested to both Connie and me that the two of us should meet and talk about the possibilities. We finally conferred on the project, and the vision took some direction. Having a heart for students, Connie shared her desire to include MCC students in the research and writing of the Inn's cameo.

I approached the students in my humanities class about this opportunity, and put the matter into their hands. As a result, these five students chose to tackle the project together: Dion Boomershine, Ashley Mahanic, Ashlee Senn, Savannah Walstad, and Sierra Walstad. Together, we drafted a plan to tour the Inn, interview Connie, meet with patrons, and do some research of the deed, documents, clippings, and other artifacts.

As part of the plan, we decided to investigate and share five primary aspects of the Inn and its history: the Clifford Lake area, the Inn itself, past and present owners, patrons and friends, and stories about its "haunting." After some deliberation, each student chose the topic that most interested her. Given my contact with Connie, I chose to assist in the writing of the Inn's history and owners' stories, as well as compile and edit the final project and add pictures with the technical assistance of my son, Jared, also a graduate of MCC and this humanities course.

On several occasions, we visited the Inn – first, for a group tour, then on individual explorations, and finally, to enjoy a meeting that Connie arranged for patrons and friends of the Inn to share their stories with Ashley Mahanic and me. The day of our tour was a spectacular, early autumn Sunday afternoon. Flowers were still blooming, the outdoor decks were bustling with chipper customers, and the glistening lake was filled with pontoon boats. Two planes were "docked" on the lake beside the hotel. On that occasion, we walked the decks, meandered through the dining rooms and kitchen, explored the upstairs rooms and hallways, and descended into the eerie basement.

Our meeting with patrons and friends included: Dorothea Ellsworth, Larry and Laura Engel, Dan Evans, Franz Mogdis, Karen Stanley, Trudy Thompson, and Tom and Patricia Wall. We simply asked everyone to share memories, stories, and thoughts about the Inn and whatever else they wanted to tell us. With laptop open and notebooks in hand, Ashley and I wrote and listened with interest. It became quickly apparent to both of us that this old structure has brought many lives together, and if its walls could speak, we would be there for a very long time. In fact, Laura Engel had so much to share, we invited her to write her own chapter on "Stories," which was also added to the manuscript.

Despite a few setbacks beyond our control, the time came for us to compile a select collection of informative tidbits, interesting stories, and historic pictures. After a phone interview with previous-owner Dyanne Eipper and a meeting with Roger Thelen, the 2011 president of the Clifford Lake Improvement Association, the project became complete. We did realize that each writer's style was a bit different, but the consensus was that we should keep the diverse styles since the project is a compilation, and the variety of approaches could serve as refreshment to the reader. Once the manuscript was fully compiled and edited, we asked Shelly Strautz-Springborn, Public Information Coordinator at Montcalm Community College, and

Kim Bell, Adjunct MCC English Instructor, to proofread and offer grammatical refinements. The end product is this saga of Clifford Lake Inn – in celebration of 130 years of hospitality to the citizens of Michigan and beyond. We express our sincere appreciation to all who contributed.

Gary L. Hauck
Spring 2012

Upper photo: Project editor Gary L. Hauck with
Clifford Lake Inn owner Connie McKeown;

Below: Hauck with Dion Boomershine, Ashley Mahanic,
Ashlee Senn, Savannah and Sierra Walstad.

Clifford Lake, Michigan (Photo courtesy of Connie McKeown)

Clifford Lake is one of Michigan's premiere all-sports lakes, with fishing, boating, canoeing, kayaking, water-skiing, camping, hiking, and cottages for rent. The 200-acre lake is bounded by West Briggs Road on the north, West Stanton Road (County Road 522) on the south, North Hillman Road (County Road 591) on the east, and North Lake Road on the west. The surrounding area also features numerous golf courses, miniature golf courses, ice cream shops, auto races, and a drag stip. The city of Greenville is 25 minutes to the south, and Grand Rapids is one hour to the southwest. Tourists have referred to the Clifford Lake area as "a slice of heaven."

Chapter 1 | Clifford Lake Area

(Ashlee Senn)

Established in 1864, Douglass became its own township in the very center of rural Montcalm County. Interestingly, it is named after U.S. presidential nominee, Stephen Douglas, a democratic senator from Illinois. Founded by Aaron Hunt and his wife, Emeline, in 1863, Douglass Township was homesteaded with 160 acres of government land. Another 40 acres of swampland were also added sometime later.

Douglass Township finally built a Town Hall in 1875. The tiny structure was just 20 ½ feet by 30 feet, and built one-half mile east of what is now known as Entrican. Before Douglass had a Town Hall, meetings were conducted in the homes of township officials.

Initially, Douglass Township was fueled by timber. White Pines were everywhere. The township eventually became home to several saw mills, owned and operated by township residents Henry Ingraham, Frank Persons, Darius Blood, a Mr. Courter and the Howell brothers. This bustling saw mill industry was big business until the early 1900s when most of the acreage of the township had been logged.

Following the booming timber and saw mill businesses, farming and agriculture became the main industry of the township. Farmers soon discovered that potatoes grew very well in the area's soil. Even today, Douglass Township is home to several potato farms.

Douglass Township is also home to Clifford Lake. By the late 1800s, this beautiful, natural resource became a resort area and tourist attraction. In 1881, a telephone line ran from Stanton to the Clifford Lake area. Also during that year Clifford Lake Hotel opened, a steamboat and yacht became permanent fixtures, and a horse-drawn "bus" brought tourists from the nearby town and county seat of Stanton to the lake.

Clifford Lake gained its name from a feeble, old man who was found dead underneath an oak tree on the lakefront property. The west side of the lake was home to the Clifford Lake Resort and the east side of the lake was home to Pine Grove Resort. Some of the early common activities were picnics, boat rides, and yacht rides around the lake. Today, Clifford Lake Inn is still a booming tourist attraction, though it is now a restaurant rather than a hotel.

The township of Douglass is much like it was 130 years ago. It is still very much an agricultural township that is home to several potato farms, and considered to be a quiet, rural community. And Clifford Lake, along with Clifford Lake Inn, has become a favored destination for residents of Michigan and far beyond.

Welcome sign to the Clifford Lake Resort Community

The Clifford Lake Improvement Association is actively dedicated to the betterment of Clifford Lake, its water quality and community.

Annual association events include: Association Meetings, a Lake-wide Garage Sale, Pontoon Parade & Lighting of the Flares (4th of July weekend), Pontoon Poker Run, Picnic and Raffle, and Golf Outing.

Clifford Lake Inn is an active participant of the Clifford Lake Improvement Association.

Aerial view of Clifford Lake and The Inn in 1957
(Photo courtesy of Connie McKeown)

The August 19, 1921, edition of the *Stanton Clipper-Herald* declared, "Clifford is becoming one of the most attractive and beautiful places to resort in the state – it will eventually beat the world in progress" (1).

Clifford Lake Hotel in 1885 (Photo courtesy of
the Flat River Historical Society)

Featured in this photo (left to right) are the Paine sisters, John Herrick, Tom Patton, Dell Paine, Leon Weatherwax, Sarah Hutchens, Nora Butchean, W. H. Bradley, Jo Culcheon, Dr. Paine, Nettie Sherwood, Carol Patton, Lizzie Johnson, and Spencer Slade. On careful examination of the photo, one will notice the tennis net on the left, and the tennis racket and ball in the hands of Spencer Slade on the far right. Sarah Hutchens (standing on grass in center) is also holding a tennis racket, waiting for Mr. Slade to serve. Tom Patton is sitting on one of two hammocks (left side of front porch), Dell Paine is reading a book (by the second post), and Jo Culcheon and Dr. Paine are playing a hand of cards (just left of the fourth post). The photo clearly shows the recreational focus of the Clifford Lake Hotel.

Chapter 2 | The Inn

(Dion Boomershine and Gary L. Hauck)

Clifford Lake Inn was built in 1881 by Lewis Smith and James W. Richards. At that time the area was called "Richard's Point." Although the Inn has gone through many owners and renovations throughout the years, it has always been a place for community socializing and good food with a beautiful atmosphere. A large, circular dance hall was erected for bands in 1914 and later used for boxing matches during prohibition and into the 1950s. The restaurant has been used for meetings and banquets throughout its history and still is today (Gustafson 176).

The structure of the building has undergone many changes. In the beginning, the Inn was a large, wooden, rectangular building with two brick chimneys located on the north and south walls. In the front of the Inn and overlooking the lake was a walk-out porch on the main and second floors with six pillars supporting it. Six long windows were also situated on the main and second floors, allowing guests to look out at the lake during the four seasons. The main floor porch sported two hammocks for lounging in the warmer weather. In the early 1900s the upstairs porch was removed to build a larger, raised porch on the main floor. On October 1, 1929, a fire destroyed most of the structure, causing $30,000 worth of damage.

This article appeared in the Greenville *Daily News* on October 5, 1929:

FIRE DESTROYS CLIFFORD LAKE HOTEL, TUESDAY

Popular Resort Structure Burns to the Ground with Loss of $30,000

Completely razing the Clifford Lake hotel and threatening to destroy the entire cottage settlement, fire believed to have started with sparks from a chimney caused an estimated loss of $30,000 at the popular lake resort about twelve miles north and east of Greenville, late Tuesday night.

The Stanton fire department was called by F. W. McConville, resident manager of the hotel, who with his family resides in the hotel during the winter months, after the blaze was discovered on the roof.

The hotel was a wooden structure and was entirely enveloped in fire before the arrival of the fire department.

Firemen pumped water from the lake to throw on the burning hotel but the impossibility of checking the blaze was quickly realized and they turned their efforts to saving the surrounding cottages.

According to the manager of the hotel, he started a fire in the furnace shortly before his discovery of the burning roof. Sparks or a faulty chimney may have ignited the shingles.

Clifford Lake is one of the popular Greenville summer resorts and the hotel was widely known as a rendezvous for local banquets and parties. No information was available today as to the rebuilding of the hotel structure by Mr. McConville. (1)

A similar article appeared in the *Stanton Clipper-Herald* that clearly identified the night of the blaze as October 1. This article added, "There was only $4,000 insurance on the building" (1). Happily, and because of the diligence and hard work of both Mac McConville and his wife, Maude, the hotel was rebuilt by the Robinson & Brady Company of Greenville, and reopened for business the following year (Gustafson 181). They continued to own and manage the establishment until 1944. An article in the *Clipper* on January 31, 1930, states:

> The new hotel surpasses the old one in many ways. It will be much larger and twice as attractive. There will be a large front room with a beautiful fireplace. The dining room will be larger and the tables will be along the sides of the room, leaving the center to be used for dancing. They have also built two private dining rooms which are very attractive.
>
> Eight large bedrooms, a bathroom and a nice hall compose the top floor of the hotel. Each bedroom has hot and cold running water, a transom above each door, and is steam heated and well lighted.
>
> A porch, which runs the full width of the hotel, adds much to its beauty. The porch is well shaded, for the hotel is built in a grove, which the firemen managed to save when the old building burned. (1)

Gustafson reports that on Friday evening, March 21, 1930, when the hotel officially reopened, patrons and residents of the Clifford Lake community surprised the McConvilles with a potluck supper in the new dining room. "After supper, L. C. Palmer suggested that Sheriff F. M. Waldo pass the hat which with the collected money was presented to 'Mr. and Mrs. Mac' on condition they return the hat to the sheriff" (181). Mack's Inn continued to be a favorite destination throughout the community.

During the next three decades, however, the old "hotel" experienced numerous changes in ownership and increasing neglect that eventually led to the building being condemned in 1975. It was purchased in 1976 by the Eipper family and many renovations began, restoring the landmark to a 1920s style. Clifford Lake Inn began to thrive once again. In 1986, the State of Michigan designated Clifford Lake Inn as a State of Michigan Historic Site. In 2010, the Inn was purchased by Larry and Connie McKeown who are working to once again bring guests in to enjoy the charm of the area either by boat, by car, or by plane.

Today, the Inn has much the same charm. The main deck is larger, with three levels overlooking the lake. It has been left uncovered with umbrella-topped tables for diners' comfort. The main entrance leads to a quaint bar and casual dining area with five large-screen televisions and decorated with both a Michigan State University flag and University of Michigan flag. The walls are adorned with pictures and newspaper clippings about the Inn's history and numerous events. One of those events, held during the month of February, is the annual winter carnival and Polar Plunge, with proceeds going to The Special Olympics. A framed article titled, "Dining Out," is John Phipps' review of Clifford Lake Inn in the May 20, 2010, edition of *The Grand Rapids Press.* Also displayed in a glass case on the wall is the Oakland Athletics baseball jersey No. 32, which was worn by Greg Cadaret in the 1980 World Series. Cadaret is a graduate of Central Montcalm High School.

The corridor at the front of the Inn leads to the porch, and a south entrance leads to a quiet dining area used for parties, meeting, and banquets. The dining area has the large fireplace and many windows for a bright atmosphere, and old-world wallpaper to add to the Inn's ambiance. A small, clean kitchen is set up with a traditional stove and brick oven to fire up the Inn's delicious artisan pizzas. The second floor is reached by a beautiful wooden staircase to the rooms above. The rooms are now used for offices and storage space and are currently under renovation, but still have many of their former features of days past. Each of the doors to the rooms still has a small transom at the top to keep warmth in or let it out, depending on the season. One former bedroom has a small opening in the wall from a dumbwaiter.

The root cellar of the building is used for storage and still contains the original charred beams left from the famous fire. It is dark and damp like most cellars and has an old, original door leading to one of the unused rooms that can only be described as "goosebump eerie." An opening in the door at eye level gives evidence of this room's possible use during the days of prohibition from 1919 to 1933. The root cellar was used as a gift shop in the 1950s.

Lakeside View of Clifford Lake Inn in the Early 20th Century (Photo courtesy of Connie McKeown)

In the early 1900s, Clifford Lake Inn was a well-known resort. Vacationers flocked from around the state to enjoy the Inn, the lake and its surroundings.

According to the *Detroit Monthly*, "Clifford Lake Hotel, built in 1881 in Stanton, a little over two hours by car northwest of Detroit in Montcalm County, is an example of the pre-turn-of-the-century clapboard resorts that once dotted inland lakes all across Michigan. The hotel is small and cozy."

"The main floor has a casual country bar and a restaurant with good food and a friendly small-town atmosphere. A bountiful country-style brunch is offered Sunday mornings. The second floor has four pretty sleeping rooms and a suite." (June 1987, 144)

Clifford Lake Inn with Main Deck

1881   Clifford Lake Inn is built in Richard's Point, later to become the owner of Clifford Lake. Chester Arthur becomes the 21st president of the United States.

1925   Mac and Maude McConnville purchase the Inn.

1929   As the country begins to enter the Great Depression, the Inn catches fire, destroying 80 percent of the building. It is rebuilt a year later.

1945   The Allies claim victory in World War II. Doc and Lillian Bruder purchase the Inn.

1955   The space race heats up between Russia and the U.S. Ed and Edie Welch begin ownership of Clifford Lake Inn.

1963   Numerous owners change the building's personality from an Inn to a restaurant to a rock n' roll bar.

Side View of Clifford Lake Inn as it Looks Today

1975 In disrepair, the Inn is condemned.

1976 The bicentennial year brings a breath of new life to the old Inn. It is purchased and restored by Norm and Dyanne Eipper.

1981 Actor Ronald Regan is sworn in as the 40ᵗʰ president, as the Clifford Lake Inn celebrates its 100th birthday.

1986 Clifford Lake Inn is designated as an official "Historic Site" by the State of Michigan.

1994 Steve and Tammie Eipper become the second generation owners of the Inn.

2010 Larry and Connie McKeown purchase the Inn and continue renovations.

Winter at Clifford Lake Inn (Photo courtesy of Connie McKeown)

Detroit Monthly carried this information during the 100-year anniversary of the Inn:

"When the Clifford Lake Hotel was built a century ago, it was part of a new community that seemed destined to become a city. A post office was established, a horsedrawn bus line provided service from Clifford Lake to Stanton, and a steamboat was launched on the lake. Fortunately for lovers of peace and quiet, urban development was not successful. The old hotel, overlooking a 200-acre spring-fed lake, is the sole survivor of all the ambitious plans. It was purchased by [Norm and Dyanne Eipper] in 1976 and gradually restored. Today it is an inn, complete with a fine restaurant, a well-stocked bar, wine cellar, and gift shop. Guest accommodations include lakeside rooms within the hotel and 26 cottages on the property. The hotel has been designated an official Historic Site by the Michigan Historical Commission." (August 1981, 50)

Interior of Clifford Lake Inn

Upper left: The Inn dining room, in what was once the front porch; **Upper right:** A new brick oven for wood-fired pizza; **Lower left:** Remnant of a dumb waiter on the second floor; **Lower right:** Fireplace in the main dining room

One menu from a bygone era included this paragraph:

Sweet Endings
**When you have finished your meal,
we would love to tell you about
our exquisite desserts...
so heavenly and sinfully sweet, they're sure to satisfy any sweet tooth!**

Clifford Lake Inn Centennial Menu - 1981
Appeteasers & Pleasers

World famous sautéed Mushrooms
Our famous delectable mushrooms are so plump and delicious, you simply must try them…sautéed with a light wine and heavy garlic butter flavor. Words alone cannot explain them!

Full order – 8.95   Half order – 6.95

Steamed shrimp
Tender pink tiger shrimp cooked just the way you like, garnished with lemon wedge and our homemade cocktail sauce.

1 lb. – 12.95   ½ lb. – 7.95

Escargot
Half a dozen jumbo mushroom caps stuffed with escargot and doused with garlic/herb butter, then carefully baked – 5.95

Potato skins
Fresh Idaho bakers fried in 100% canola oil (low saturated fats…the 'good for you' fryer oil!), smothered with bacon bits, green onions, Colby and Jack cheese, served with our special dressing

Full order – 6.95   Half order – 4.95

Buffalo wings
Lightly battered and fried chicken drumsticks, coated with our own hot sauce, then served with homemade bleu cheese dressing. Can be ordered mild or hot (and we mean HHHOOOTTT!) – 5.50

Chicken tenders
Tender, all-white strips of chicken breat, fried till golden and accented with your choice of sauces   - 4.95

Fiesta dip
Nachos too messy? Try our Fiesta Dip. Layers of seasoned beef, refried beans, Colby & Jack cheeses, lettuce, tomatoes, jalapenos, and a cloud of sour cream – 4.25

Outrageous onion rings
Our famous beer-battered onion rings. For the onion ring enthusiast/ connoisseur. Large Spanish onion rings beer-battered and lightly fried to perfection in canola oil – 3.95

(We use cholesterol-free oil in all our frying!)
Don't miss the
Root Cellar gift shop
Downstairs

Upper left: Stanton Business Men's Banquet 1926; Upper right: Hotel guests and their catch;

Middle left: Owners Maude and Mack McConville (1925-1944); Middle right: Owners Edith and Edward Welch (1955-1963);

Lower left: Owners Norm and Dyanne Eipper in period costume, celebrating the Inn's 100th anniversary (1976-1996). (Photos courtesy of Connie McKeown)

Chapter 3 | Innkeepers

(Sierra Walstad and Gary L. Hauck)

The journey of the previous owners of Clifford Lake Inn has been a long yet rewarding one. Since the land was purchased in 1855, the property has changed ownership several times. **Carso Crane** was the first to make a contribution to Clifford Lake Inn's history. On December 15, 1855, he purchased the lot from the United States on which Clifford Lake Inn would later be built. However, ownership of the land would be passed a few more times before the building would be constructed. Ownership was passed to **Samuel B. Peck** in 1870, and then to **Edwin Potter** in 1876, however, Edwin's ownership was short lived. Ownership passed to **Lewis Smith** later that year.

While under the ownership of Lewis Smith, the land amount increased. In 1880, Lewis Smith went into partnership with **James W. Richards**, who had serious plans for the location. James Richards obtained 1 ½ more lots, platted the land as the "Plat of Point Richards" and built Clifford Lake Inn, which opened for business in 1881. Shortly after, James Richards took complete ownership of the land and the Inn, and Lewis Smith was no longer mentioned.

After only two short years of owning the land and the newly built Inn, property ownership was transferred to **George F. Dunn** in 1882, then to **Michael E. Fanning** in 1883, and then to **Clarence W. Chapin** in 1884. Between 1884 and late 1912, there were many claims to the Inn and its lots; however, no clear ownership was recorded due to a misplacement of the deed. According to A. M. Gustafson in *Douglass – A Michigan Township*, **Theodore Willebrand** owned the property from 1898 to 1901, and "saw the possibilities of a first-class resort" (173). He reportedly spent several thousand dollars to make improvements and modernize the hotel.

On December 30, 1901, **Fred D. Briggs** obtained the Inn, and then sold it to his manager, **John Campbell** in 1912, who in turn sold it to **Edwin J. Hammersley** that same year. Also in 1912, Briggs purchased one third of the property with a loan from the Bank of Stanton. He passed away in 1916. Briggs left the property to his widow, Mabel, and three minor children. However, the State Savings Bank of Stanton foreclosed on the widow and three children in 1917. In the meantime, **Ulysses G. Hayden** owned the Inn from 1914 to 1917, and made several renovations, including the addition of a circular dance hall built around a large oak tree near the Inn. The grand opening of the remodeled Inn was held on June 20, 1914 and included "good speaking, singing, ball games, races…and dancing in the new hall in the evening" (Gustafson 178). Music was provided by the Sidney Brass Band. Hayden also "planted several thousand fish in the lake including lake trout" and held July 4 extravaganzas that included "a balloon ascension, a motor boat race, foot racing, skating and dancing in the new hall, sack and potato races, greased pole climbing, a baseball game, a big display of fireworks on the lake, and a brass band to play all day" (Gustafson 178). However, in June, 1917, ownership of the Clifford Lake Inn was transferred to **Royal A. Hauley** and **John W. Dasef**.

On December 30, 1918, **Charles L. Spaulding** purchased the Inn with a mortgage of $4,000.00 and seemed to have had an ambitious plan in mind. On February 5, 1919, Spaulding re-mortgaged $3,000.00 to buy five more lots and platted it "Spaulding's Plat."

Between the time of the purchase of five more lots and 1925, ownership was once again a mystery. However, it has been said that **Rose Toleson** and her then husband, **Art Taylor**, had owned the Inn before selling it to **Mac and Maude McConville** on October 6, 1925.

The McConvilles took pride in their good food, entertainment, and hospitality. In 1926 the radio orchestra from the Grand Rapids radio station was engaged and during the 1927 season it was Walter Swartz and his Silver Bay Orchestra. It was billed as the only orchestra in the state of six persons playing 17 instruments and a vaudeville favorite.... McConville booked the orchestra at the highest price ever paid a six-piece orchestra in northern Michigan. Mack's Inn became a popular place for dinners and banquets. (Gustafson 180).

During their time owning the Inn, a devastating fire occurred (see chapter 2), damaging a substantial amount of the building. Fortunately, the Inn was rebuilt the next year by the McConvilles, and restored in even grander style. In 1944, the Inn was purchased by **"Doc" and Merle Chapin**.

Since being built in 1881 by James Richards, many of the previous owners have contributed in some way to keep the historical building, as well as the successful business, up and running and have a story to tell. Fortunately, a few were able to share their stories. Doc and Merle's story is kept alive due to their daughter's memory of Clifford Lake Inn.

Gwen Chapin Shultz was 19 when her parents made the decision to leave their farm in Grandville, Michigan, and purchase Clifford Lake Inn. "Doc was in ill health and ready to retire," she muses, "and when Merle became aware that Clifford Lake Hotel was going to be up for sale, she believed the resort would be where Doc could retire and rest." Being that Merle was "a hard worker, an excellent cook, and a true optimist," according to her daughter, "it was obvious that she would be successful, and talked Doc into buying the hotel."

Doc and Merle bought the Inn in 1944, and the couple and their family learned the restaurant business the hard way. While their oldest son, Norman, was overseas in the infantry fighting in Germany, the rest of the family had obtained jobs at Clifford Lake Inn. Doc ran the bar with help from the regulars, and Howard, Jr., their youngest son, was in charge of renting out boats and waiting tables. Merle cooked for the hotel guests and for banquets of up to 50 guests, and her sister, Rose, who had previously owned the Inn, helped with cooking and cleaning. Gwen quit her job as a secretary of a department head in an aircraft parts factory in Grandville, Michigan, and helped her mother at the Inn.

After two and a half years of owning the Inn, Merle came to realize that it was not just about feeding people and making them comfortable. Also, Doc's health had declined, forcing them to move back to Grandville. The Inn was sold to **Alexander and Lillian Bruder** in 1946, and Doc Chapin passed away in 1949.

Ownership was transferred to **Ed and Edie Welch** in 1955. During their tenure, the Inn was transformed into a restaurant and "rock n' roll bar." **Jack and Arlene Wall** took over from 1963-1971. However, the Inn declined considerably during the next few years and was sadly condemned in 1975. While it seemed as though the building was unfit for business, its potential was recognized by Norman and Dyanne Eipper in 1975.

Norman and Dyanne Eipper were two real estate brokers from Lansing, Michigan, who knew just what they were getting into when they purchased the Inn in 1976. They spent months renovating the worn down Inn and happily state, "it eventually paid off." It was during their ownership in 1986 that the State of Michigan designated it as an official Michigan Historic Site. After 20 long years of satisfying hard work, their love and respect for the building and the business was passed on to their son, Steve Eipper, in 1996.

Steve Eipper took the business into his hands with pride. He maintained the historical beauty of the Inn and being a culinary institute graduate, he was able to keep a successful business for over a decade. However, in 2010, Steve gave **Larry and Connie McKeown**

the chance to own this historical establishment and Connie now runs the business.

Having moved through the ranks of human resources for several years in a manufacturing, retail, and business environment, Connie made her way from Flint to the Montcalm area 18 years ago when she met her husband, Larry McKeown. Larry has owned a body shop business in Sheridan, Michigan, for 22 years. As the two began to date, Clifford Lake Inn became a favorite destination for them. For Connie, this began a romance with both Larry and the Inn.

When the two decided to marry in 2002, they shared a strong belief in working and living in the same community. Larry would obviously maintain the body shop and now also supported Connie's commitment to "women in business." Connie enjoyed working with people, and joined the human resources department at Wright Plastic Products in Sheridan. Here she gained significant additional experience in finance and personnel management. After 10 years, however, she was ready to own and establish her own business as well, having developed professionally from all aspects of human resources to executive management.

Much to her delight, when the previous owners of Clifford Lake Inn decided to sell the business in 2010, she cashed in her retirement and secured additional financing to purchase the Inn on March 31 of that year. Papers were signed at 10 a.m., and she reopened the facility at 4 p.m. on the very same day! "That first year was quite a year of learning," Connie shares. "It's been a lot of work, and there were a lot of hidden maintenance costs, but I love the challenge and I love what I do."

From the beginning of this venture, the new owner had a clear vision of the Inn's mission: "We are strong supporters of our community, and want to give back all that we can. My goal is to offer a venue and events for the local community where our folks can enjoy good food, great service, and affordability." She continues to explain, "Hopefully, the Inn will not only be a destination for birthdays, weddings, anniversaries, and other family events, but a regular gathering spot for community programs, fundraising events and celebrations." Some of these have included the Central Montcalm Community Foundation annual "Big Bash" fundraiser event, the annual Polar Plunge event day to benefit Special Olympics, the Stanton Women's Club annual themed dinner fundraising event, an annual Triathlon to benefit the Central Montcalm Girls Basketball program, Central Montcalm High School Top Academic Banquet, and Leadership Montcalm. "I would like to include banners from all the area schools," McKeown muses. "I already have a University of Michigan banner, but I might need to add a Michigan State banner just to be neutral!" Both are now hanging side by side.

Connie also made a commitment to somehow make the Inn fresh while not losing the historical ambiance. In 2011, the facility added two lower deck levels facing the lake, a wood-fired pizza oven, four TVs in the bar to create more of a sports bar atmosphere, new plumbing and electrical service, and additional outdoor aesthetics. Along with carefully maintained flower gardens, preparation is underway for the Inn's own herb garden for use with its menu. This would complement the commitment already in place to use primarily local fresh fruits and vegetables.

With new ownership comes a combined perspective of building on the established past, and setting some new directions. With that in mind, Connie took some new directions with a "hands-on" management style, slight shift in professional culture, and open book policy. These changes have been met with different perspectives by its long-term customers who experienced the Inn for 34 years under its previous managements. "Changing the guests' perception of an established Inn is always risky business. But ongoing development is inevitable," she states. This is also true for staff. Currently, the Inn employs a staff of 15 – a chef, four sous chefs, two cooks, servers, and dishwashers, and a general manager. The objectives for the staff include a measure of flexibility, creativity, accountability and team-building.

A variety of distinct features made their way to the Inn through the years – a gift shop in the basement, pool table, juke box, and the incorporation of personal or public artifacts. While most of these are now gone, some old and new artifacts remain, and the desire to create a balance between casual and elegant pervades. Under the new ownership, other goals are also in place. These include the use of technology such as social network sites and emails to give bi-weekly event "blasts," live music every Tuesday and Thursday evening from Memorial Day to Labor Day (using local musicians), Murder Mystery Dinners, Talent Nights, Ladies' Luncheons, Book Clubs, Guest Speaker Lunch 'N Learns, Travelogues, Christmas in the Country, Carriage Rides and more.

Top row left: Clifford Lake Inn in the early 1900s; Top row right: Old Clifford Lake houseboat;

Second row left: Side view without shutters in 1927; Second row right: After the fire of 1929;

Third row left: The round dance hall in 1935 located 200' north of the Inn; The Inn in 1975;

Bottom row left: Aerial view of the Inn in 1957; Aerial view of Clifford Lake.

Connie McKeown, the current owner of Clifford
Lake Inn states, "Time stands still here."

Today's customers of Clifford Lake Inn arrive by many means!

Chapter 4 | Patrons and Friends

(Ashley Mahanic)

Since 1881, The Clifford Lake Inn has had a very long and interesting history. The Inn experienced many changes but what has remained the same is the loyalty of the Inn to its community and the community's loyalty to Clifford Lake Inn.

The "old days" at Clifford Lake Inn were lively times with a round dancing hall that doubled as a skating rink and even a boxing arena during the days of prohibition and into the 50s.

Local author Dorothea Jorgensen Ellsworth has lived on Clifford Lake for 67 years and has many vivid memories. One of those memories dates back to 1935 when Clifford Lake Inn hosted a pageant. It was held outside and had a medieval theme. Dorothea went with her father to watch her two older sisters, Iola and Hazel, perform. She recalls how everyone wore elegant costumes and that one of her sisters played the role of a herald. She wore a puffy-legged outfit and carried a long horn that she blew before delivering an important message. According to Dorothea, the pageant was directed by Agnes Hunt from the Gleaners Organization.

Another memory Dorothea shares is one that her late husband, Vernon Ellsworth, used to mention about his childhood on the lake. As a child, Vernon raised worms. He would row across the lake on Sundays to the Inn to sell his worms to the fishermen. One Sunday afternoon, while he was selling his product, he saw some of his family members having a picnic on the lawn in front of the Inn. While visiting with them, someone yelled, "There's a baby in the lake!" He ran to the lake and grabbed the baby, which happened to be one of his cousins. Thankfully, he got there just in time.

Larry and Laura Engel tell the following story about Larry's grandfather: Prior owner, Mac McConville, prided himself on maintaining a peaceful, respectable establishment. He did this with the aid of a blackjack, which he kept behind the bar. One evening, Larry Engel's grandfather, Robert "Rob" Engel and his wife, Grace Neitzel Engel, were seated at a table in the bar area. Apparently some kind of altercation broke out in the area where they were seated. Mac resorted to the trusty blackjack to restore order. Unfortunately, his aim was bad. He hit Grace instead. Rob Engel was incensed that Mac blackjacked his wife. He never again patronized the Inn until the McConvilles sold the business to the Chapin family and left the area.

Larry Engel also recalls another saga from when the McConvilles owned the Inn. It was evidently during this time that a parrot lived at the Inn as well. Larry recalled that it did speak, but the only word he can remember it saying was "Mac," the name of the owner. This same bird also loved to consume alcoholic beverages that the patrons would give him! After too many drinks the parrot had been known to fall of his perch and nap on the bottom of his cage! Such was some of the local entertainment at Clifford Lake Inn.

Tom Wall spent many years at Clifford Lake Inn, living in the upstairs while his parents owned the Inn. He remembers coming home from school to find older men in the bar playing euchre. Sometimes, if they had an uneven amount of players, they would have him fill in. He also recalls how his friends would always want to come over because they could go to the kitchen to make burgers and fries and grab a Coke whenever they wanted. However, he jokingly states that since he was raised on "restaurant food," it was always special for him to go to a friend's house and eat "homemade food." As he muses on the many responsibilities that his parents had as owners, he remembers that "it was always a very busy time for my parents. They would be up all night cleaning up after the late night crowd left and be right back at it first thing in the morning cooking for their

Sunday breakfast buffet. But I had a lot of fun, and carry many fond memories of life at the Inn."

Although times have changed, Clifford Lake Inn is still focused on individual customers as well as the community. Currently the Inn holds many events that benefit the community. Every year, Clifford Lake Inn holds a Triathlon the third week in August. The event consists of three sporting events including a one-half mile swim, followed by a nine-mile bike ride, and ending with a two-mile run. All of the proceeds go to area school sports programs. Central Montcalm High School's girls' basketball team won the trophy in 2010 and 2011.

During the second weekend in February, the Inn holds its annual Winter Carnival. As a part of this event, volunteers are invited to join in the yearly Polar Plunge. More than one hundred participants jumped in both 2011 and 2012. The Winter Carnival also features cross-country skiing, ice fishing, ice sculptures, and fireworks. Money raised from this event goes to the Special Olympics.

Clifford Lake Inn also sponsors a family event called "Christmas in the Country." Begun by Larry and Connie McKeown, this celebration features family pizza specials, cookie decorating, carriage rides, and stories by the fire. This is a "Toys for Tots" event and the Inn serves as this community's location for the collection of items to be distributed to underprivileged children during the holidays.

The owners of Clifford Lake Inn are happy to invite their patrons to hold their special events at the Inn, too. Franz Magdis tells about his 70th birthday party that was held at the Inn, where he can be found on most evenings. On this special occasion, some 50 invited guests enjoyed a buffet style dinner. The theme of this birthday was a "comedic roast," with a number of participants "roasting Franz" with humorous stories.

Over the years, the quaint setting of Clifford Lake Inn has witnessed engagements, baby showers, anniversaries, birthdays, family parties, class reunions, and school gatherings. In the words of one satisfied customer who registered comments online, "Great atmosphere. Sit on the patio, nice dining room, or at the bar. Good food, good drinks, friendly people."

Interestingly, the Inn is quickly becoming a destination for wedding ceremonies -- either inside, or on the lawn. As a recent bride expressed, "The Lake made a fantastic backdrop for our wedding ceremony!"

Recent set-up for a lakeside wedding at Clifford Lake Inn

Clifford Lake Inn Bar

"I have been going to the Clifford Lake Inn all my life. The mushrooms are a favorite for everyone. The Brick fired pizzas here are awesome too. They are as good as any others in West Michigan" (Robert T., Clifford Lake Inn reviews).

"We ate lunch there on the way out of town to wrap up our little vacation. I had the pecan crusted trout with 'fruited' rice, and my husband had the seared walleye. Both dishes were wonderful. The server told us that the kitchen was staffed by three recent culinary school grads, and you could really tell. It's hard to find a place in rural mid-Michigan that has contemporary, healthy and delicious food, something we really take for granted back home in Southern California. This was a delight, and we only wish we would have known sooner as we would have eaten here several times during our stay.

"BTW, I also had the molten chocolate cake for dessert. It was very tasty and the perfect size, not too big at all, the size of a cupcake. It came in at $4.95, so compared to what we're used to back home, it seemed very reasonable and far superior to similar dishes found at chains" (Karen N., Clifford Lake Inn reviews).

Christmas at Clifford Lake Inn

(It was in this room we met with patrons to hear their stories)

Franz Mogdis is a daily patron of the Clifford Lake Inn and bar. He remembers the changing image and clients of the Inn over the years, and has also witnessed evidence of the "unseen guests." Dan Evans remembers years when they had to cut through 18 inches of ice on the lake to clear an 8-by-8-foot or 10-by-10-foot opening for the Polar Plunge. Larry and Laura Ellsworth Engle recall coming to the round dance hall to hear "Fred Webb and his Nighthawks." The dance hall was built around a giant oak tree, and the bandstand was several feet above the dancers. Tom and Patricia Wall remember the screened in porch, and the time Tom's dad opened it up. Tom lived in the Clifford Lake Inn when his parents owned it from 1963 to 1971 (Jack and Arlene Wall). Trudy Thompson speaks of the pontoon parades, and a car that once drove across the frozen lake to the Inn. Dorothea Ellsworth calls the Inn, "the hub of Clifford Lake." She has lived for 67 years in the Clifford Lake Community and writes novels of its culture.

This Sign Hangs in Clifford Lake Inn

Chapter 5 | The Haunting

(Savannah Walstad)

Clifford Lake Inn has had many followers over the years – some young, some old. But just how long have some been visiting? The Inn has been around since before patrons could get in a car and drive there; before one could pick up the phone and call to see how late it was open. As easy as it is for us to walk in and order something new on menu, eat our fill, and walk back out, some believe that we may be joined by others who find it a little too hard to leave this place. Some believe it; others may not. For those who do, Clifford Lake Inn is more than just a restaurant or bar to the owners, staff, and guests. It is home to some who have passed, but stay at the Inn in presence.

What do I think? Just because you can't see them or hear them doesn't mean they aren't around. And if you're lucky they make their presence known to you. This place has been around longer than you and I. It's been through multiple owners, weathered many years, opened doors to thousands, made a comeback after fire tried taking it down, and was a hideaway during the prohibition (still containing the original door used on the room where the secretly kept alcohol was served). The Inn was a bed to sleep in when it was a hotel, and a place to find neat knick knacks when it had its own gift shop. Now it operates as a restaurant and bar, but is so much more than that.

From the outside, it looks like nothing that would be haunted. Between the new and bustling outdoor deck, community engagement, fundraisers, book clubs, private parties, and more, the present owners keep it lively and glowing. But, don't turn out the lights or you could be in for a surprise! The Inn looked amazing during my tour, and nothing gave me the "creeps" on the main floor; it was the basement and top floor that randomly made the hair on the back of my neck stand. This was not so much because I could feel something there, but the fact that so much was original, like the old style wash sinks in the rooms upstairs, the beams and wood boards in the basement. You don't know who had lived there or who had died there, or whether it was a homey, warm place, or if you were standing in the very spot something dark could have very well happened.

With such an extensive history and few records to document the happenings at the Inn, it is difficult to explore events that may contribute to the "haunting" of the Inn. So, if what you know of the Inn's hauntings isn't enough to make you feel intrigued, just imagine the secrets that could have gone to the grave with those who previously were a part of the Inn's life. The Inn is celebrating 130 years. A lot can happen in that amount of time. A lot of information has been lost in the process. Papers can wither and pictures can burn away, one man's story is completely different after being told by the 20th different person. Some believe that if a spirit chooses to remain, remain it shall.

So, even though they aren't still alive, might they give us keys to unlock doors to some of that lost and misguided information that has been hidden away and confused over time? The Inn has a multitude of rooms, all with their own story, but the oddities of a few catch your attention. One has a dark cubby hole tucked in a corner where it is said paranormal experts found recordings and evidence of the Inn's ghostly longtime visitors. In another room, at the top of the wall, there's a small cupboard looking door, but when you open it, it goes nowhere. It is one of those things that makes your mind wander. Was this really a door to a dumb waiter?

No one knows exactly who these "ghosts" are or where they came from, but Clifford Lake is a small-knit little community of its own. So, it is highly rumored that it's just not the Inn that has experienced hauntings. One name that surfaces is of a girl or woman named Megan. No one is sure of her relation to the Inn, or who she may even be, but she has evidently made her name clear to more than one person. She's just one of the said unknown numbers of others who linger around, partaking in the Inn's constant activity. To probe further, owner Connie McKeown brought in paranormal investigators.

Right there for all to see who visit the Inn is a plaque on the wall recognizing Clifford Lake Inn as an officially haunted establishment by G.H.O.S.T. Paranormal Investigators. These investigators have now made several visits to the Inn and claim to have identified activity from more than one ghost. They don't just hit the jackpot in one certain room, either. From the basement, to the bar on the main floor, right to rooms on the third floor, they get striking evidence of activity. Of course, they have high-tech equipment to help them when it comes to hearing, seeing or feeling any of the spirits who inhabit the Inn. The phenomena that happened and that are unexplained come out of nowhere, and just plain scare the observers. Trust me, there's plenty of that, too!

I was lucky enough to meet one-on-one with the investigators and get an inside look at all they discovered. The group was able to give me some interesting information on what they experienced. Here's an inside look on a bit of what they dealt with, told by Kyle Carter, G.H.O.S.T.'s tech manager.

Two or three times during the night, several of us (myself included) clearly heard someone walking down the short hallway that goes between the staircase and the women's bathroom. We had our monitors set up just around the corner from there, and each time that it happened (I heard it twice) they were clear enough that I was certain one of the team was about to come around the corner. I know that two other members of the team heard footsteps in and around the upstairs bathroom, the one still under construction. At one time during the night, I was sitting in the room with the two mirrors in it with another member of the team, Mindy. I had purposely set the two mirrors so that they were facing each other, just for the ambiance of it. At one point, we were asking questions, hoping to evoke answers, when one of the mirrors moved. It didn't move far, just sort of turned a little bit, but the scraping sound it made against the carpet as it did so was very distinct. Sadly, we did not get anything from the audio that was running in the room at the time. (Personal interview)

When meeting with the investigators, I brought up a story that Connie passed on to me from one of the lake's residents, a self-acclaimed psychic. She told Connie that she gets the name, Megan, in her investigations of the Inn. G.H.O.S.T. team members had never heard this story and when I brought it up and mentioned the name, Megan, it instantly caught their attention. In one of their recordings from an earlier investigation at the Inn, they had asked what the being's name was, and a very specific response of "Megan" was heard in the reply. To this day, no one knows who Megan is or what exactly she has to do with the history of the Inn. But, she has made herself known to more than one person.

G.H.O.S.T. also told me a story about doing a recording outside of the basement room where the alcohol was kept and served during prohibition. According to the investigators, spirits find one of the recording devices quite irritating, and in this case the ghosts made that known. In the recording from that room, the paranormal experts say they overheard voices of what seemed to be two men. After a momentary hush, they heard one of the spirits utter, "All is clear," and in that instant the recording device shut down completely and the brand new batteries in it were completely drained!

These are just a few of the intriguing occurrences that Clifford Lake Inn has experienced. Many of the long-time patrons have witnessed similar phenomena. And, obviously, the staff has as well. For instance, a woman bartender went to reach for a wine glass hanging in a rack above the bar, but within an inch of physically touching it, the glass burst into shattered pieces. There is no explanation at all. Those staying after hours to clean up have heard voices, or had lights been turned on and off on them in several rooms. Even the owner has witnessed these happenings for herself. "Sometimes as I lock up the Inn for the night and begin to drive away, I will see lights come back on that I just turned off. It's actually happened several times," Connie McKeown reports. "We have a set routine of turning off all the lights at night, and we always double check, but even others have been the last to leave the Inn only to look in the rear view mirror and see lights turned back on."

A group of students from Montcalm Community College who comprise "The GHOST Club" (Ghost Hunters of Sidney Township) has also visited Clifford Lake Inn for investigations. Debra Alexander, the club's advisor, shows a high-tech, night-vision video recorded in the basement. It clearly shows a well-defined white mist moving from one room into another. The video was taken by a guest investigator - Mark Oberlin, who joined The MCC Ghost Club at Clifford Lake Inn on December 11, 2011.

All of this could be going on one room over from you where you're eating dinner, and you would never know. The roar of dishes clanging, foods sizzling, and the chatter of fellow customers, drown out some of the smaller noises. So what you may think is a worker walking around upstairs just might not be! So you see, you are one of many guests at Clifford Lake Inn.

The following article appeared in the online edition of *The Daily News* of Greenville, Michigan, on January 19, 2012, posted by Ryan Schlehuber:

STANTON — No one knows how long "Ed" and "Megan" have been a part of Clifford Lake Inn. Many people may not believe they exist.

But on Jan. 14, many visitors of the 131-year-old inn were talking about them.

"Ed" and "Megan" are two apparitions that roam

through the lakeside eatery, according to owner Connie McKeown. She confirmed her belief that the inn was haunted through recent paranormal investigations.

Those findings were revealed to the public at a "Haunting Unveiling" event last Saturday and will again be displayed at a second public showing at 6 p.m. Friday, Jan. 20.

"Clifford Lake Inn is haunted, based on our evidence we collected in March and again in October," said Scott Sheldon, lead investigator and founder of GHOST, a paranormal investigation group from Mount Pleasant.

Of the past 24 places GHOST investigated, Sheldon ranks Clifford Lake Inn in the top five in most active. He said Mount Pleasant's Broadway Theater is the most active, followed by the Whitefish Point Lighthouse in the Upper Peninsula.

High-tech evidence

Using highly sensitive equipment that captures the slightest sound, movement or temperature change, Sheldon's seven-member team was able to capture up to eight EVPs (electronic voice phenomenon) during the team's March visit.

One EVP captured a little girl's voice stating her name, "Megan." Sheldon said one of his flashlights then went dead and another EVP was recorded with a little girl's voice saying "all clear."

During the team's October visit, which was at night when the inn was closed, they witnessed a mirror moving by itself and caught another EVP of what sounded like two men talking in the basement with lights going on and off, said Sheldon.

"We caught at least three different voices during our visits," he said. There was never a time where the team felt threatened, according to Sheldon. "I really do feel like they'd rather avoid people, that they're just happy hanging out at the inn," he said about the apparitions.

Another paranormal investigation group, Taunting Whispers of Greenville, captured video evidence of apparitions at Clifford Lake Inn. "We caught quite a few things during our investigation," said Sandy Bogart, who, with her brother, Mark Overlin, operate Taunting Whispers.

Bogart said Taunting Whispers will have a monitor with a live feed to the inn's "cubby" room upstairs, where there's been a lot of activity, at Saturday's "Hauntings Unveiled" event.

Owner is a believer

McKeown wasn't a firm believer in ghosts before she and her husband, Larry, purchased the Inn in March 2010. But with experiences of encounters continuously happening among her and her staff, she quickly started to believe in the afterlife.

"What I find the most interesting of all of this is that fact that I've never felt scared or nervous with this place or these apparitions being here," McKeown said. "Any evidence we found was very friendly, which intrigued me even more, especially with the great deal of history connected to this place."

McKeown believes "Megan" may have been the daughter of a linen keeper at the inn and 'Ed' was an employee who may have died in a fire at the inn in 1930. She hopes to find more information not only on "Megan" and "Ed" but the inn's history itself.

McKeown said a guest — and an apparent psychic reader — visited the inn last summer and informed her and general manager Kim Hirkaway that she could feel many spirits in the inn. She was the person who confirmed "Ed."

"She told me that Ed was still here, apparently trying to make amends for starting the fire in the 1940s" as an apparition, McKeown said.

She has been trying to locate the woman, hoping to invite her back for more readings, but has yet to find her.

Since news of the paranormal investigations went public, McKeown has had many people and other paranormal investigators contacting her about Clifford Lake Inn's hauntings. "It's been crazy, the response I've had," McKeown said. "One lady sent me a letter warning me that there is a demon coming. I expect there will be a lot of paranormal followers and groups willing to come out here." (1)

Interestingly, the only fire we know about is the one on October 1, 1929, that was accidently set by the owner, caused by sparks from the furnace. According to all news accounts, no one died in that fire.

A more recent article by Cory Smith from *The Daily News* dated Monday, April 9, 2012 states that the "G.H.O.S.T. paranormal group certifies Clifford Lake Inn as haunted." Smith continues:

> The question of whether spirits from the afterlife are among us here on earth has lingered for centuries, but according to one paranormal investigation team, Clifford Lake Inn in Stanton is officially haunted with their presence.
>
> G.H.O.S.T. Paranormal Investigations, based out of Mount Pleasant, officially declared the restaurant haunted earlier this year. Their findings, despite what you may believe, were discovered using equipment and tactics similar to what you might see on several paranormal television shows, but without the theatrics.
>
> Paranormal shows such as "Ghost Adventures" on the Travel channel and "Ghost Hunters" on the SyFy network fit everything together in an exciting half-hour or hour time frame. Minus the theatrics designed to attract viewers for ratings, members of G.H.O.S.T. set out to investigate Clifford Lake Inn in a professional manner looking for similar results.
>
> "What you see on TV isn't completely wrong, just more (exaggerated)," G.H.O.S.T. team member Kyle Carter said during an investigation of Clifford Lake Inn in March. "There are four of us here tonight and we'll break into teams of two and explore the building. We'll have audio recordings set out and if we're lucky one of our cameras will catch something."
>
> Investigating the Clifford Lake Inn
>
> During the group's recent trip to Clifford

Lake Inn in March, Carter said he and his fellow team members were hoping to gather more evidence to strengthen their case of the restaurant being haunted, or perhaps debunk some of the evidence they discovered in their previous two visits.

The team uses equipment and technology exactly similar to what you would see on any paranormal television show. From Electronic Voice Phenomenon (EVP) devices to Electromagnetic Field (EMF) detectors, the group approaches their mission seriously in the late hours of the night, which start as early as 8 p.m. and can last until sunrise.

"The idea (with an EVP) is that you leave a voice recorder running in a location and when you listen to it later you can hear voices or sounds that weren't there to your own ears at the time," Carter said. "We were able to find several examples of that the last time we were here."

The group's investigation in March was their third time searching through the restaurant, and according to Carter, there was plenty of evidence suggesting spirits haunt the historic building.

"The last time we were here we heard footsteps, very, very loud footsteps," he said. "One of the mirrors in the upstairs bedroom moved while I was sitting next to it, which was awesome."

According to group member Scott Sheldon, the group has confirmed two voice recordings off of EVP's, which they believe are former employees currently haunting the restaurant.

"I know there was a disgruntled employee who worked here long ago named Edward," Sheldon said. "On our first visit we captured an EVP where we asked 'What's your name?' and we did get a response of the name 'Edward.' We asked again later in the night and also heard the name 'Megan.'"

Carter said those two employees were likely involved in a fire that burned down the restaurant many years ago.

"The building itself is like 130 years old, it has a long history," he said. "At one point in the past the building did burn down and supposedly one or two of the spirits here are believed to have started or died in that fire."

Three Michigan buildings labeled "haunted"

Clifford Lake Inn joins the Broadway Theater in Mount Pleasant and the Wexford County Museum in Cadillac as three locations that G.H.O.S.T. has officially labeled as "haunted." The group has investigated more than 30 locations having only been together for just under two years.

According to Sheldon, it takes more than a whisper and a chair rocking in the wind to declare a location officially haunted.

"There's a difference between being haunted and having paranormal activity," he said. "We look for three separate pieces of evidence; audio, video and personal experiences. If we can come out of (an investigation) with good, solid evidence from those three groups, we can declare a location haunted…." (1)

Despite these "evidences" that have been reported, many other faithful patrons of the Inn remain skeptical of the existence of these unseen visitors. In a personal letter dated February 12, 2012, local author Dorothea Ellsworth writes, "I was surprised when I read about the ghosts that were supposed to have made the place spooky. I don't believe a word of it!" Later in a phone conversation on April 28, Laura Engle stated, "I don't believe in ghosts, and do not believe the Inn is haunted. However, it is still a wonderful place to experience, and will always be one of my favorites."

The upstairs hallway of Clifford Lake Inn

"A Haunting? Some of the visitors to the Inn report lights turning on and off and sounds or 'sightings' of a little girl. No one seems to know who she was" (*The Daily News* online).

"[General Manager Kim] Hirkway remembers two guests who were visiting family in the area, a grandmother and granddaughter, who came to the inn for dinner and apparently could feel, hear and even see the presence of ghosts while they were there. 'We don't know who they were but they definitely told us a lot about who and what we have here,' Hirkaway said" (The Daily News, January 7, 2012).

The eerie basement of Clifford Lake Inn

STANTON — Many residents and visitors have enjoyed visiting and returning to Clifford Lake Inn, a resort destination for 131 years. According to new paranormal investigative evidence, some people have never left.

Inn owner Connie McKeown and General Manager Kim Hirkaway [invited] the public to meet with two groups of paranormal investigators [to] unveil evidence that the historic inn is frequently visited by apparitions during a "Haunting Unveiling" event on Saturday, Jan. 14. The event [included] psychic readings for a nominal fee, "spirited special dinners" and an introduction to Michigan's newest vodka, Ghost Vodka, made in Detroit.

A charred beam in the basement of Clifford Lake in from the fire of 1929

Mid-Michigan Paranormal Investigators of Mount Pleasant and a paranormal investigation club from Montcalm Community College [revealed] their findings of ghostly encounters from overnight research earlier last year. "We found this is a very active place," McKeown said. "It's all been very fascinating and interesting."

McKeown said she and her staff have had many encounters, from hearing footsteps, seeing lights go on and off after the inn is closed and hearing the water from a faucet upstairs constantly turn off and on. "Our motion detector constantly goes off," she said. "There's been a lot of activity in the basement, too." (*The Daily News,* January 7, 2012)

The "speak-easy" door in the basement of Clifford Lake Inn

Chapter 6 | Stories

(Laura J. Ellsworth Engle)

The following are human interest stories from Clifford Lake Inn and the Clifford Lake Community. Some of these are my own reflections, and some have been told to me by Gwen Chapin Schulz, my husband, Larry Engel, and by Dorothea Jorgensen Ellsworth. Together, they show the human fabric that has woven the community and Inn together over the years.'

Clifford Lake Hotel Memories (As told by Gwen Chapin Schulz)

The three years from 1944-46 were adventurous ones for "Doc" (Howard Chapin, DVM), his wife, Merle and their family. Doc was in ill health and ready to retire, but the farmers whose animals he cared for wouldn't allow it. When Merle became aware that Clifford Lake Hotel was going to be for sale, she felt the resort would be where "Doc" could retire and rest.

Her sister, Rose Toleson, had owned the hotel with her then husband, Art Taylor, years earlier (1930's?) before selling it to "Mac" McConville and his wife Maude. Merle was a hard worker, an excellent cook, and a true optimist. She talked "Doc" into selling their farm in Grandville, Michigan, and buying the hotel in 1944.

"Doc" ran the bar with the advice and assistance of the local "regulars" - farmers Ed Fritz, Carlton Engel, Frank Jensen, and many others. The family's oldest son, Norman, was overseas in the infantry fighting in Germany. Their youngest son, Howard, Jr., was 14 and their daughter, Gwen, was 19.

Howard was put in charge of renting boats and also waiting tables. Merle's sister Rose, who lived on Dickerson Lake, helped with cleaning and cooking, and Gwen, who had quit her job as secretary to a department head in an aircraft parts factory in Grandville, was her helper.

Merle cooked for hotel guests and for banquets of up to 50. Chicken dinners were the main meals served, with an occasional weekend fish fry. Fishermen would put their week's "catch" on ice and have Merle fix a big fish dinner on Friday. Alice Fritz, daughter of Ed, was the main kitchen help.

After dinner, the big dining room was cleared for dancing on weekends. The bar was usually busy with the "regulars" and weekend cottagers, and the dances were well attended. One particular and memorable one turned into a near riot when one of Vic Black's brothers thought his wife was the target of a "snide" remark.

A fight started and, as it grew, someone (I think Art Black) fell through the glass French doors separating the dining room from the living room and nearly cut off his ear. The fight continued until Merle grabbed a blackjack from behind the bar and waded in to stop it. Someone decided she needed help and got the fight stopped before the local sheriff, Ray Disbrow, arrived.

"Fred Webb and his Night Hawks," a musical combo from Stanton, entertained at the square dances held in the round dance hall built around a giant oak tree just north of the hotel. Their bandstand was a platform built around the tree several feet above the dancers.

One such dance was memorable when a member of the celebrating party over imbibed and insisted on driving home. His girlfriend and others tried to stop him, but to no avail. Norman, Chapin's oldest son, was home on leave from the army and heard the commotion. When he found out what was going on, he went to the man's car, opened the hood, and tore out some wires -- problem solved!

Gwen was asked to remember any special events that occurred during those three years. Her main memories involved the antics of her younger brother, "Hud," (Howard Jr.'s nickname) and his buddy, Art Adams. One dance night, he opened a window slightly and, from the dark outside, he shot peas at the dancers. When a group of angry men went out to look for him, Hud and Art hid in a car in the parking lot and pretended to be "neckers." Merle found out about it and had Gwen sneak the boys upstairs and made them stay there until the Inn closed for the night.

Another time, a group of the neighborhood kids took the big eight-seater rowboat through the channel and to the far west end of the lake. It was a moonlit night, ideal for stealing watermelons. The farmer whose garden they were raiding caught on and threatened to shoot them. They scrambled back to the boat and made their getaway, eating melons along the way and tossing the rinds overboard. In the morning, a trail of rinds led directly to the Inn! Local girl, Audrey Miller Malling, was part of this adventure.

I think, after 2 ½ years, Merle came to realize that owning the hotel constituted a lot more than just feeding people good food and making them comfortable. Also, Doc's health had declined even more and she decided they must move back to Grandville. They sold to "Doc" Bruder in 1946 and "Doc" Chapman died in 1949. However, the memories of Clifford Lake Hotel never left them.

More Clifford Lake Memories (As told by Larry Engle)

Larry Engel's aunt, Irene Engel Russell, grew up during the Depression. She left school after completing the 8th grade to enter the workplace. Irene, like many young people of her generation, was a hard worker by necessity, but she always made it a point to play as hard as she worked.

Two of Irene's closest friends in those days were Lorraine Miller and Beatrice Evans. They lived in the same neighborhood and spent a lot of their leisure time together. Like Irene, Lorraine and Beatrice enjoyed being young and having a good time.

One evening, when they were attending a dance, three young guys asked them to go for a ride. They left the dance and soon ended up in a deserted lovers' lane. These fun loving girls were probably not prudes by any means. But they did not like the direction the evening's activity was taking.

Irene gave her date a strategically placed punch that may or may not have caused permanent damage. She said afterwards that her preemptive action "calmed him down a lot." It should it also be noted that her rather colorful description of him as a date has been omitted to make the account of their adventure acceptable to general audiences.

Realizing that the girls were not being nearly as cooperative as the young men had hoped, they ordered the three Clifford Lake area friends out of the car and drove away. The girls were left to find their own way home in the darkness. Needless to say, they were not any happier about the way the evening had ended than the guys were.

An opportunity for revenge presented itself sometime later. Lorraine and Beatrice were attending a dance at the Clifford Lake Hotel's round dance hall when they spotted a familiar car in the parking lot. It was the same car the would-be seducers had driven when they sped the girls to the lover's lane. Luckily, it was a distinctive model and color making it easily recognizable. Lorraine and Beatrice climbed into the car, released its parking brake, and rolled it down a steep bank into Clifford Lake.

Aunt Irene claimed not to have been with her two friends when this happened. It was, however, the very kind of prank she would have devised. Even after being questioned on several separate occasions about the events involving the "drowning" of the car, Irene steadfastly stuck to her claim of noninvolvement. Maybe the whole story will never be revealed.

The Clifford Lake Hotel Parrot (As told by Larry Engel)

Larry Engel remembers that a parrot resided at the Clifford Lake Hotel, probably at the time Mac and Maude McConville owned the business. This would have been prior to 1944, the year that the McConville's sold the business to Howard (Doc) Chapin and his wife, Merle.

It seemed that the parrot did talk a bit. But the only word Larry recalled him uttering was the word "Mac," the name of the hotel owner. What was much more interesting to Larry than the bird's proficiency with the English language was its fondness for alcoholic beverages. The customers would give the parrot samples of whatever they happened to be drinking. At some point, the poor parrot would fall off his perch and "sleep it off" on the floor of his cage.

During this same time period, the hotel also featured another interesting drawing card that would have appealed to children of Larry's age at the time. (He would have been 7-9 years old in the early 1940s.) Outside the hotel, adjacent to the parking area was a caged squirrel. Larry didn't think he was particularly tame, as he was seemingly never allowed out of the cage. It has not been recorded that the squirrel had a drinking problem. It could have been a legal issue; the parrot could well have been over 21, but the squirrel certainly was not!

Memories of the Clifford Lake Hotel Staff

Larry Engel's mother, Pauline Rasmussen Engel, worked at the Clifford Lake Hotel for some 20 years. She retired in 1964 to care for her mother-in-law, Grace Neitzel Engel, who was suffering ill health.

One memory that Pauline related involved an accident that occurred when she was working in the kitchen. At the time, she was checking on a large turkey that was baking in the oven. She pulled out the rack to inspect the turkey. Unfortunately, the last person to remove that rack had replaced it upside down. Consequently, the rack did not stop and lock part way out, but came out completely. Both the rack and the turkey ended up on the kitchen floor!

Pauline was devastated about this error. Fortunately for her, Doc Bruder, and not his extremely tidy wife, Lillian, was on duty at the time. He came into the kitchen.

"What shall I do, Doc?" Pauline wailed.

"Pick the darned thing up, put it back in the oven and don't tell Lil," he ordered.

That's exactly what Pauline did. She didn't feel that anyone would be put at a risk for disease by doing this because Lillian was a true neat-nik. Pauline always swore that anyone could eat off Lillian's kitchen floors at any time. Unbeknownst to those diners who ordered turkey later that evening, that's more or less what they were doing!

Clifford Lake Hotel Owner "Mac" McConville

Mac McConville evidently prided himself on maintaining a peaceful, respectable establishment. He did this with the aid of a blackjack that was kept behind the bar. One evening, Larry Engel's Grandfather, Robert "Rob" Engel, and his wife, Grace Neitzel Engel, were seated at a table in the bar area. Apparently some kind of altercation broke out in the area where they were seated. Mac resorted to the trusty blackjack to restore order. Unfortunately, his aim was bad. He hit Grace instead. Rob Engel was incensed that Doc had blackjacked his wife. He never again patronized the hotel until the McConvilles sold the business to the Chapin family and left the area.

Celebrated Patrons

My husband, Larry, and I recently visited the attractive Clifford Lake home of Vernon and Dorothea Ellsworth, two of the most celebrated patrons of Clifford Lake and its old Inn. Larry wanted to talk to Vernon about his military service (which was featured in the Hodges-Archer Newsletter at an earlier date.) My mission was to get a brief, personal history of the lives of my kinfolk, and a sample of life in the Clifford Lake Community over the years.

Dorothea was born Dorothea Jorgensen. Her mother's side of the family was a mixture of northern European nationalities. But both of her father's parents were natives of Denmark.

Dorothea is very proud to be one-half Dane.

Vernon's great grandfather, Joseph Ellsworth, was granted an 80-acre tract of land on the north side of Clifford Lake as a reward for his Civil War service. As has been reported in earlier editions of the newsletter, Joseph married the former Julia Jenkins. Joseph and Julia's son, William Joseph Ellsworth, familiarly known as Billy Joe, married the former Agnes Enness. One of their sons, Clyde, was Vernon's father. Vernon's mother was the former Frances Crawford. Clyde and Frances purchased the 80-acre farm from his father, Billy Joe.

After World War II ended, when people were interested in recreation again, Clyde and Frances platted off the lakeshore and sold lots. People from Detroit, Lansing, Grand Rapids and

Greenville bought lots and constructed cottages. Clyde saved one lot for himself and gave a lot to each of their seven children: Vernon, Beatrice, Russell, Ben, Mary Ann, Arlene, and Bill. Ben and Mary Ann lived too far away to enjoy their lots, so they sold them to Vernon so he could build a cottage to sell. Vernon's grandson, Dallas Bell, and Dallas's wife, Kim Bell, both adjunct instructors at Montcalm Community College, live in the house now. It is rare that a property remains in the same family for nearly 150 years, but that is exactly what has occurred in Vernon's case.

Like many other couples in the past 60 plus years (including Larry and me) Vernon and Dorothea met at the Rainbow Gardens Roller Skating Rink in Crystal. Vernon loved to roller skate and visited the rink twice a week. At the time of their meeting, Vernon was employed at Federal Mogul in Greenville and Dorothea was teaching at the Mt. Hope School, a rural school located north of Carson City. They were married by the Rev. Cornelius in the Lakeview Methodist Church Parsonage on March 11, 1944.

Dorothea relates that the roller skating rink at Crystal burned one week after their 1944 wedding. For a time, the skaters had to relocate to the Crystal Palladium. The Palladium was a huge attraction at that time. It featured a bar on the ground floor and a huge dance hall on the upper level that occasionally played host to many big name bands of the era. A new rink was later constructed and the skaters had their own facility once again.

Although Vernon and Dorothea were married in 1944, they had to delay establishing a permanent home until Vernon could complete his military obligation. Those were the days of World War II, and millions of men were faced with putting their lives on hold for the duration.

Dorothea stayed with her school-teaching career while Vernon was in the service. She recalls that he once received a leave from service and came home to surprise her. She was teaching at the rural

Mulholland School when a loud knock came at the schoolroom door. Dorothea thought that someone must be very angry with her to rattle the door that loudly. The door opened, and it was Vernon. He said. "School's out for the day, kids. Go on home." They went.

After his discharge from the service in 1946, Vernon began a huge project -- that of building a home for his wife and himself. Dorothea relates that up to that time, Vernon had never attempted to build anything more sophisticated than a lean-to or a fishing shanty. The basement was completed late in 1946 and the Ellsworths moved in. Dorothea's father allowed Vernon to cut all the lumber needed for construction on their new home from his woods, which was a lot of work, but provided a big savings in material costs.

No electricity was yet available on the north side of Clifford Lake due to a wartime scarcity of materials and manpower. All water had to be pumped by hand from the well in the basement. In 1947, this area finally got its electrical service, which made lives a lot easier for Clifford Lake residents. City dwellers seldom think about it, but rural residents face the added task of pumping their own water from beneath the ground. Electric pumps are required to supply that most precious commodity to each of the plumbing fixtures in the home. Without electricity, water taps don't dispense any water and toilets don't flush.

To add to Vernon's construction woes, many building materials were still rationed and very scarce. For instance, he had a difficult time constructing the hardwood floors in the upstairs of the home. When the hardwood was available, inevitably a portion of it had to be returned because it was defective. Then the waiting began until another supply was available. It wasn't a matter of going to Lowe's or Home Depot and loading up everything needed for a given project in one trip, as weekend "do-it-yourselfers" are able to do now.

Some bright spots existed in those days. Prices for the building materials were lower. The Ellsworths have a beautiful view of Clifford Lake from their large living room windows.

Dorothea recalled that the four windows cost a total of $48 when Vernon first installed them in 1947. They were replaced in recent years with more energy efficient panes, which Dorothea says, "cost a lot more than $48!"

Dorothea and Vernon subsequently became parents to two children, Sherolyn in 1946, and Joseph in 1949. Dorothea invented the spelling of Sherolyn`s name because she wanted a daughter that she could call Sherry. Joseph was selected because Vernon liked the name. It wasn't until later they discovered it was also a family name of long standing.

Their oldest child, Sherry, had suffered from severe asthma from childhood. Softball, swimming, and roller skating (her dad's favorite sport) seemed to be some of the few pastimes that did not aggravate her asthma. Her life was tragically cut short in 1981 when she succumbed to congestive heart failure, a condition brought on by her asthma and the medications used to treat it.

The Ellsworths have been blessed with four grandchildren: Dallas and Mark Bell, Jesse Joseph, and Annette Ellsworth. Their great-grandchildren are: Terran and Victoria (Tori) Ellsworth, Mackenzie Bell, and Jamie, Blake, and Elle Schmitt.

Although a stroke has slowed Dorothea's physical mobility, her mind in 2012 is still razor sharp. If she does happen to forget some small detail, she can readily recall it with the assistance of a diary she has kept for many years. Vernon provides invaluable assistance to Dorothea in their home.

Vernon spent his working years at Gibson Refrigeration in Greenville, while Dorothea was a busy housewife. In later years she wrote five books for the Dream Series that reflects life in Montcalm County during the 1800s: *No Time to Dream, Give Me My Dream, Dreams Do Come True, This Dream is Real,* and *The Long Awaited Dream.* Although the setting for these stories is said to be her Aunt Agnes Jorgensen Comden's Pleasant Hill neighborhood, Dorothea confides that much of the imagery comes from her own Clifford Lake community.

The Ellsworths recently celebrated 65 years of marriage. Their anniversary picture in the local paper prompted some 130 congratulatory cards. They are no doubt the most celebrated patrons of Clifford Lake and its old Inn.

Epilogue

Ever since the days when horse-drawn buggies brought resorters to enjoy the charm of the area more than 130 years ago, Clifford Lake Inn has been continuously providing hospitality to those who visit. It remains a touchstone of history and of progress.

The first telegraph line was stretched from Stanton to Clifford Lake resort on October 1, 1880, but instead of a telegraph instrument as intended, a telephone was put into operation. It took, however, until February 22, 1881, for the first conversation to pass over the wire. When the U.S. Post Office opened in 1881, the town was known as Richard's Point. Clifford Lake Inn was constructed and opened for business. A horse-drawn "bus" line transported passengers from Stanton to Clifford Lake. The cost of a round trip fare was a whopping five cents. A steamboat also was launched at the lake that same year.

The Inn has gone through many transformations since 1881. It has experienced destruction by fire, multiple owners, a condemned state of disrepair, renewal, restoration, and changes of style. Despite the many challenges along the way, the Inn not only remains a staple of Montcalm County, but has been declared a State of Michigan Historic Site since 1986. More recently, teams of paranormal experts have also declared the old Inn, "haunted."

Today, owners Larry and Connie McKeown continue the tradition of offering delicious meals in this quaint lakeside setting just a few miles west of Stanton. The kitchen uses locally grown vegetables, locally produced cheeses and Michigan ingredients wherever possible. If you ask those who frequent the Inn for Rotary Club meetings, leadership summits, the annual Polar Plunge, school awards ceremonies, family celebrations or just an afternoon or evening of enjoyable dining, you'll hear new stories that now become a part of the ongoing historical record and heritage of Clifford Lake Inn.

Clifford Lake Inn

If floors and walls could only talk
And tell of those who once did walk
The halls of the Inn at Clifford Lake
Perhaps your heart and mind would take
A journey there yourself!

One hundred thirty years or so
The young and old would come and go
For food and drink and pleasant rest
Searching for the very best
And now it's time for you.

Some tales are told of "extra guests"
Who might be on a special quest
To linger at the Inn still more
(Though traveling through some distant shore)
And join you at your side.

When all is said and all is done
And history's tales have come and gone
A new beginning sets its mark
While looking back it will embark –
The Inn at Clifford Lake
G. L. H.

Works Cited

Alexander, Debra. Personal communication. 17 Apr. 2011.

Carter, Kyle. Personal Interview. 16 Dec. 2011.

"Clifford." *Stanton Clipper-Herald.* [Stanton, MI] 19 Aug. 1921. P. 1.
Print.

"Clifford Lake Hotel." *Detroit Monthly.* [Detroit, MI] June 1987. P. 144.
Print.

"Clifford Lake Hotel Anniversary." *Detroit Monthly.* [Detroit, MI]
August 1981. P. 50. Print.

Clifford Lake Improvement Association. *Bylaws of the Clifford Lake
Improvement Association.* Clifford Lake, MI: CLIA, Amended
11 July 2009. Print.

Clifford Lake Improvement Association. Meeting Minutes. 4 June 2011.
Typescript.

Clifford Lake Improvement Association. *The Clifford Lake Chronicle.*
Clifford Lake, MI: CLIA, Winter 2011.

"Clifford Lake Inn Centennial Menu." Douglass, MI: Clifford Lake
Inn, 1981. Print.

Clifford Lake Inn official website. Web. http://www.cliffordlakeinn.
net/

Clifford Lake Inn reviews. Web. http://www.yelp.com/biz/clifford-lake-
inn-stanton

Ellsworth, Dorothea. Group interview. 8. Nov. 2011.

Ellsworth, Dorothea. *No Time to Dream*. Stanton: Ellsworth, 1987. Print.

Ellsworth, Dorothea. Letter to the manuscript editor. 12 Feb. 2012. Typescript.

Engel, Larry. Group interview. 8 Nov. 2011.

Engel. Larry. Personal communication. n.d.

Engel, Laura. Group interview. 8 Nov. 2011.

Engel, Laura. Telephone interview. 28 Apr. 2012.

Engel, Laura. Faxed letter to the manuscript editor. 21 Dec. 2011. Typescript.

Engel, Pauline Rasmussen. Personal communication. n.d.

Evans, Dan. Group interview. 8 Nov. 2011.

"Fire Destroys Clifford Lake Hotel, Tuesday." *Stanton Clipper-Herald*. [Stanton, MI] 1 Oct. 1929. P. 1. Print.

Gustafson, A. M. *Douglass, A Michigan Township*. Douglass Township, MI: Gustafson, 1982. Print.

McKeown, Connie. "Clifford Lake Inn." Menu, n.d. Print.

McKeown, Connie. Personal interview. 19 Sep. 2011.

Mogdis, Franz. Group interview. 8 Nov. 2011.

Oberlin, Mark. Personal video. 11 Dec. 2011.

Ravell, Richard G. "Abstract of Title in Town Eleven North, Range Seven West." Montcalm County, MI., n.d. Typescript.

Schlehuber, Ryan. "Clifford Lake Inn to Unveil Paranormal Findings" *The Daily News* [Greenville, MI] Web. 7 Jan. 2012. http://thedailynews.cc/2012/01/07/clifford-lake-inn-proving-to-be-a-haunting-good-time-%E2%80%94-unveiling-paranormal-findings-jan-14/

Schlehuber, Ryan. "Public to Learn More At Clifford Lake Inn's Second Paranormal Event." *The Daily News* [Greenville, MI] Web. 19 Jan. 2012. http://thedailynews.cc/2012/01/19/public-to-learn-more-at-clifford-lake-inn%E2%80%99s-second-paranormal-event/

Schulz, Gwen Chapin. Personal interview. n.d.

Smith, Cory. "G.H.O.S.T. Paranormal Group Certifies Clifford Lake Inn as Haunted." *The Daily News* [Greenville, MI] Web. 9 April, 2012. http://thedailynews.cc/2012/04/09/

Thelen, Roger. Personal interview. 20 Mar. 2012.

Thompson, Trudy. Group interview. 8 Nov. 2011.

Wall, Patricia. Group interview. 8 Nov. 2011.

Wall, Tom. Group interview. 8 Nov. 2011.

About the Authors and Editor

Ashley Mahanic is in her second year at Montcalm Community College, studying early childhood development and education as a paraprofessional. She is a native of Cedar Springs, Michigan, and is interested in all aspects of humanities.

Dion Boomershine is a returning student to Montcalm Community College pursuing paralegal studies. Upon her graduation from MCC, she will be attending Ferris State University, and possibly law school. She enjoys photography as a hobby, and spending time with her daughter, Regan.

Laura J. Ellsworth Engel graduated from Montcalm Community College in May of 1971 with an Associate Degree of Arts & Sciences. She and her husband, Larry, are celebrating 48 years of marriage this year. Laura began working in the Stanton post office as a clerk in 1959 and held that position until she was sworn in as Stanton's first female postmaster in 1971. Her hobbies include reading, history, and playing the organ.

Ashley Senn received her Associate of Arts degree in Business Administration from Montcalm Community College, and is currently enrolled in the bachelor's program at Ferris State University, majoring in health care management. She enjoys sewing, photography, and reading, and spending time with her husband, Gavin, and children: Lauren, Breylon, Brynlee.

Savannah Walstad, a third-year student at Montcalm Community College, looks forward to a career as an animal control officer. She enjoys riding, training, and barrel-racing horses, and likes to shoot, skate, and volunteer at local animal shelters. Savannah also enjoys shopping and spending time with her family.

Sierra Walstad is in her third year at Montcalm Community College with the career goal of becoming a speech and language pathologist. She is also studying customer relations. Sierra likes making discoveries in culture and history, and enjoys music and the arts.

Gary L. Hauck (Ph.D., Michigan State University), is Dean of Instruction and Faculty at Montcalm Community College, where he also teaches humanities. He is a board member of the Flat River Historical Museum and the Heritage Village Association, chairman of the Montcalm Area Humanities Council, and a member of the Mid-Michigan Arts Council and Montcalm Area Art Association. Gary also serves as the co-chair of One Book One County – Montcalm, and has served on the board of the Montcalm Area Reading Council. He is the author of sixteen books.